501 SURVIVAL TIPS FOR MEN

Making Your Way in a World Full of Women

501 SURVIVAL TIPS FOR MEN

Making Your Way in a World Full of Women

Craig Hartglass

A Citadel Press Book
Published by Carol Publishing Group

A Citadel Press Book
Published by Carol Publishing Group
Citadel Press is a registered trademark of Carol Communications, Inc.
Editorial Offices: 600 Madison Avenue, New York, N.Y. 10022
Sales and Distribution Offices: 120 Enterprise Avenue, Secaucus, N.J. 07094
In Canada: Canadian Manda Group, P.O. Box 920, Station U, Toronto, Ontario
   M8Z 5P9
Queries regarding rights and permissions should be addressed to Carol Publishing Group, 600 Madison Avenue, New York, N.Y. 10022

Carol Publishing Group books are available at special discounts for bulk purchases, for sales promotions, fund-raising, or educational purposes. Special editions can be created to specifications. For details, contact Special Sales Department, Carol Publishing Group, 120 Enterprise Avenue, Secaucus, N.J. 07094

The tips presented in this book are for entertainment purposes only. Neither the author nor the publisher assumes any responsibility for the use or misuse of information contained in this book.

Manufactured in the United States of America

10   9   8   7   6   5   4   3   2   1

Library of Congress Cataloging-in-Publication Data

Hartglass, Craig.
    501 survival tips for men : making your way in a world full of
  women / Craig Hartglass.
      p.   cm.
  ISBN 0–8065–1504–X (pbk.) :
      1. Men—Life skills guides—Humor.   I. Title.   II. Title: Five
  hundred one survival tips for men.
  PN6231.M45H335   1994
  818′.5402—dc20   93–42155
                                                         CIP

PREFACE

Yes, I know it's usually the publisher who tries to slap the disclaimer on any controversial, explosive, or libelous material that could end up with a deranged Book-of-the-Month Club fan gunning him down in the company garage, or even worse, in a big fat lawsuit. But, being the magnanimous kind of guy that I am, I thought I'd beat 'em to the punch.

This book is not—repeat NOT—for the average "play by the rules" kind of guy. So if you, or the loved one that you're thinking of giving this book to, own suspenders, drink chocolate milk, or know mother's phone number by heart, just put this book back on the shelf. It's not for you (or him).

This book is—repeat IS—for the guy who's sick of "playing by the rules" and getting nowhere. Just take a look around...some men seem to have the secret to life. You know them—they're easy to recognize. They glide through life effortlessly, everything falling into their laps. We see them laughing confidently at cocktail parties—without a care in the world—as one hand absent-mindedly brushes back wisps of hair and the other casually snakes around the waist of his latest girlfriend. These guys are seldom the best looking, or the best dressed, or even the richest, yet they always seem to be surrounded by adoring women, countless business opportunities, and even more adoring women. Is it genetic...an unattainable gift, doled out by nature? Hardly. They just know something most guys don't...

While our society may praise decency, honesty, and integrity, it chooses to reward individuals that...let's just say, fall somewhat short of these lofty goals. And as for women, they may *say* they want "nice guys who they can talk to," but the world is filled with "nice guys," and the only girls who will talk with them have 900 numbers and charge by the minute. No, things are truly not as they seem.

And these guys know all that. They don't play by the same "rules" as everybody else. In fact, if you were to watch them closely, you might conclude that they had "a rule book" all their own—for getting the most out of life. And you'd be right.

After years of careful observation I managed to isolate and chronicle the *501 Survival Tips for Men* (1,002 should the first 501 become a bestseller)— the very tips responsible for success. And you now hold them in your hands.

But use them wisely. Remember, our free society flourishes on its members own sense of personal responsibility for their actions. And to this end I hereby absolve myself (okay, and my publisher) of any such responsibility should any of the survival tips herein backfire (particularly should jail, bodily harm, or irate feminist actions result). And as for lawsuits, might I suggest you turn to Tip Number 1....

1.   Never trust a lawyer.

2.   When choosing a bank, go with the toaster. While interest rates rise and fall rapidly, an appliance dies slowly.

3.   Don't overlook your office as a place to meet women for sex.

4. Never get your fingernails polished, unless you're a chick, or a transvestite. Then go for Flaming Red.

5. Always cheat on tests. In ten years *nobody* remembers algebra but your grade transcript will be with you forever.

6. Learn to speak another language. Foreign people are usually talking about you—so find out what they are saying.

7. Get into the habit of chewing gum; nothing hides booze breath better. If you chew it all the time, no one will notice any change the next time you really need it.

8. Keep your girlfriend on a short leash. Those collars and wrist bands with the little studs are nice, too.

9. If you want to become a crazed psychopath, drive around all day listening to talk radio. If you already are a crazed psychopath, call in.

10.   Make friends with someone who owns a pool.

11.   Get a dog. Chicks love dogs.

12.   When playing Monopoly always insist on being the Banker. It's the position that affords you the most opportunity to cheat. Real Estate Broker is next but not as good, since properties run out soon after the start of the game. Art imitates life.

13.   Money can't buy happiness. But if you're bent on being miserable.... It's best to be miserable on a tropical island, sipping a frosty cold drink, surrounded by bikini-clad babes. Money *can* buy *this*.

14.   Act as if your phone is always bugged.

15.   Never treat a woman like a piece of meat. By this I mean don't brush her with barbecue sauce and then toss her on the grill. There are laws against that sort of thing.

16. Drink a little more heavily from time to time. You'll be surprised how often a high threshold comes in handy.

17. If you find yourself better off financially than your neighbors, invite them over to see your new big-screen TV, stereo, computer, and VCR.

18. If you're considering marriage, try to visualize her when she lets her hair color grow out, her tan fade, and her diet slip. That's what she will look like as your wife.

19.   Don't pay attention to the news. It changes every day.

20.   Learn to play cards well—then pretend you're just a beginner.

21.   Get an unlisted phone number.

22. Never hit on your best friend's wife. Always try to get her to make the first move.

23. When having a party, buy cheap booze. Pour it into the empty bottles of top brand names. Your guests will never know the difference. As an added bonus some will even make fools of themselves by insisting it tastes so much better than "lesser" brands.

24. As a guest at an exclusive restaurant, always order the most expensive dish on the menu. Not to do so insults your host, mocking his ability to pay for it.

25. When handling the money of others, reckless abandon is best.

26. Pretend to be interested in cultural happenings.

27. Keep a straight face when saying things like: "Your best girlfriend, Nancy, has enormous breasts? Really, I hadn't noticed."

28. Try to get in an afternoon nap—preferably on company time.

29. The final word on penis size. It matters. A lot.

30. When visiting friends, don't wipe boogers on their walls, at least not while they're watching.

31.   When you're in a hotel in a strange city, the bellman—for a surprisingly small fee—can usually offer assistance in procuring the services of a prostitute.

32.   Take the money you would spend on your kid's education and buy them a nice car instead. They will appreciate it more and you'll have money left over for yourself.

33.   Be nice to wealthy relatives.

34.   Don't drive drunk. Amphetamines are much better for long trips.

35.   If she insists on foreplay, invite another couple.

36.   When choosing a wife, look at her mother. That's your spouse in twenty years.

37.   Start a membership at an out-of-town video store under an assumed name. Rent your porno tapes there.

38.   Keep a gun in your car. And a shovel in the trunk.

39.   Always make friends with guys with tattoos, missing teeth, or vacant stares. These people can save your life. Or end it, should you piss them off.

40. Never laugh at a girl in the gym. Remember, she might look like a heifer at 5 in the afternoon while pedaling an exercise bike in leotards. But put her in a darkened bar after midnight, wearing a low-cut dress, drink a half-dozen beers—and you're looking at a Penthouse Pet.

41. A rule of thumb when dining out: The bigger the breasts, the bigger the tip. Plus extra if she flirts with you.

42. Break chocolates in half before eating them. If you find jelly or mint inside, squeeze them back together and return them to the tray. Try again.

43. A little knowledge can be a dangerous thing. Be safe—drop out.

44. Urinating in the eggnog is hardly ever as funny as it seems at the time.

45. Always insist on a prenuptial agreement—unless your intended is extremely wealthy, in which case say you don't believe in that sort of thing. Besides, having one isn't necessary if you're *really in love*.

46.   Attend school reunions. Arrive in a limousine, prefera-
        bly a stretch with a TV and a bar.

47.   When hiring a secretary, remember what's really impor-
        tant: *Anyone* can type, but how does she look in heels
        and a miniskirt.

48.   Never criticize your boss. Well, not to his face, at least.

49.   Get as many credit cards as you can. Pay your balance on one card with a cash advance from another. When the second bill comes in, pay it with an advance from a third card. Then cancel the first card and apply for another one. Repeat the cycle. You can live well beyond your means without ever having to dip into your own pocket.

50.   Never buy the same present for both your wife and your mistress.

51.   Always encourage lesbian experimentation among your girlfriends.

52.   Vote for the crook who's not yet in office.

53.   Never buy a second-hand car. Hot-wiring takes only a few minutes to learn, but it's a skill that lasts a lifetime.

54.   Deny everything.

55. Try to pick a mistress with the same first name as your wife.

56. When your wife asks what you're thinking about, never, ever, be truthful.

57. Tell any women you meet that you don't have a phone at home.

58.   The worse you treat them, the better they like it.

59.   If you want an air bag in your car, bring your wife along for a ride.

60.   Pick a doctor with a liberal prescription policy. Doctors who don't insist on annoying checkups before writing prescriptions are best.

61.   Pay gambling debts before bills. Collectors for the former are far more fierce.

62.   Always get the hottest girl you can find to cut your hair. You're not going to look like Don Johnson anyway, so you might as well enjoy yourself for half a hour.

63.   When a woman asks if her thighs look fat, the rule is: If it's just after sex, tell her the truth. If it's just before sex, lie.

64.   Staying at a hotel? Take binoculars. Lots of people forget to draw their blinds.

65.   Develop a friendship with a boat owner.

66.   Wear expensive imported boots.

67. Stay in shape. The years go by quickly, and remember, if you get fat but don't get rich, too, you'll never get any young girls.

68. Never break cleanly. During lonely evenings a comforting "old friend" can claim certain privileges. An "ex" gets none.

69. A woman on the rebound is both fair game and easy prey.

70.   The chase is funner than the catch. But not by much.

71.   Complain often of an ailing back. The "favors" this will get you out of are too numerous to mention, but they include moving furniture.

72.   Make friends with a few cops.

73.   Change flat tires for strange women. There's no such thing as a "feminist" in a dress and heels with a flat tire. These women become real females again, and often they'll even be grateful enough to have sex with you. Generally speaking, the nicer she's dressed, the better your chances. It also helps if you cut yourself in the process.

    It doesn't have to be anything serious, but you do need to shed *some* blood. This triggers a basic biological reaction. Upon seeing blood, she'll shift into her nurturance mode and rifle through her purse looking for some tissues and Band-Aids. Pretend it hurts as she wipes the blood clean, but don't overact. This is a good time to give a compliment. Try to avoid any mention of her breasts or legs, since that would shoot her right back into her feminist mode. Though women *do* want you to notice such things (as evidenced by all the money they spend on cosmetic surgery), you're not supposed to notice them right away, or at least not mention them if you do (we're still not real clear on that).

Safe topics for a compliment include her smile, her wound-dressing ability, her personality, etc. Comparing her to a beloved older female relative (especially your mother or your aunt) is particularly good. If the compliment goes well, at this point she should be a boiling mass of hormones. Make your move.

74.   When attending a bachelor party, let the stripper think you have never seen one before. That is, if you don't mind getting stuck with the job of removing her panties while she sits squirming in your lap.

75.   Never tell a female about the true goings on at a bachelor party. Someday she will be married to some poor slob who will want to go to one. It could be you.

76.   At a bachelor party drink heavily and encourage others to do the same. If *everyone* gets involved in things they hope to forget the next day, they most likely will.

77.   Strike up a conversation with someone at a lunch counter. When you go up to pay the cashier, say that your friend is paying for your lunch. When she asks you what friend, wave to him across the room. He'll wave back, and she'll think he's "okaying" the arrangement.

78.   Disconnect the odometer on new cars.

79.   If on a date you spend an amount equivalent to the cost of a prostitute's services, you are entitled to sex. (The prostitute must be of a caliber similar to your date. You can't compare a toothless $5 whore when your date is more along the lines of a midrange call girl. Be fair.)

80.   Keep a safe deposit box for items your wife would best not see.

81.   Keep a P.O. box for private mail.

82.	If planning a convention, choose a place that would best serve your business needs—provided it has booze, gambling, and loose women. Remember: Many men are counting on you for the only fun they might have all year.

83.	Keep a loaded gun near your bed.

84.	Never refer to movies as "films" or "pictures"—unless you are talking to an attractive bohemian-type woman. In which case *always* refer to movies as "films" or "pictures."

85. If you develop any early warning signs of a fatal disease, ignore them. They'll probably go away on their own.

86. Tell a woman with small breasts that you're an ass man.

87. Excessive alcohol will remove cholesterol from the blood.

88.   Develop a friendship with your boss's boss.

89.   Don't pay lawyers' bills.

90.   When a large estate is involved, divorce takes a back seat
        to murder. In eight to ten years you'll be a free man, *with
        everything*. Plus interest.

91.   In the case of divorce, seek full custody of the children. Your wife will give up everything to get the kids, leaving you a free and single bachelor with a house, two cars, and all the money.

92.   Never pay your last two months' rent.

93.   Don't be rude to men wearing pinky rings, especially in Las Vegas.

94. Get passports and papers made with phony names.

95. Always use a condom when having sex with a prostitute—unless she tells you she's disease free.

96. Become friendly with all neighborhood kids. they are a
great source of low-cost labor, and it will impress your
dates.

97.   Smoke cigars.

98.   Drink bourbon or whiskey either straight or with ice—
        never in anything from a blender, or called "sour."

99.   Don't report additional income.

100.   Never ask to see your F.B.I. file.

101.   Keep a change of clothes in the trunk of your car.

102.   Don't ever make a pact with the devil by writing him a letter and setting it on fire. Not even for fun.

103. Fly first class. The food is better, you get more room, and the stewardesses, thinking you are rich, will be much more inclined to have sex with you.

104. Women are impressed by three things: money, looks, and a long johnson. If you don't have any of the above, you might try developing a personality.

105. When shopping for big-ticket items, let it be known that a large discount gets your cash, while the sticker price gets your credit card.

106.   Never drink while on the ski slopes—the chair lift is far
         more appropriate for cocktails.

107.   Buy real intellectual books at garage sales. Highlight
         certain passages; then leave the books open—around
         your apartment—for people to pick up and leaf
         through.

108.   Work hard—as long as people are watching.

109.   Goof off a lot.

110.   Never quit a job. Make them fire you so you can collect
        unemployment.

111.   If real estate prices go down, don't pay off your
        mortgage. Let the bank have the worthless house, while
        you spend a few years living rent-free as they try to
        evict you.

112.	Don't grow your hair long. The few girls it will attract aren't worth all the loan officers, cops, and rednecks it will offend.

113.	Looking for sex? Go to church. Lots of women go there to meet nice guys—they'll never suspect a thing.

114.	Pick out a woman's weak point and compliment her on it. Nothing gets her panties off faster.

115. Squelch your children's dreams from an early age. It's better if they get used to facing adversity early. Besides, do you really think you're going to be able to pay for medical school?

116. Don't forget about your girlfriend's friends. Usually they'll be jealous enough to go to bed with you.

117. Playing the stock market: Buy low, sell high.

118.   Have life insurance—on your wife and kids.

119.   Hiring a maid? Remember: She'll be bending over to pick things up and reaching on tiptoe to put things away. You can always hire someone else to tidy up if necessary.

120.   Don't cavort with criminals. Do your business, then leave.

121. Never compliment a women on her large breasts until you are looking at them in the flesh.

122. Avoid cat people—they're weird.

123. Always pick up hitchhikers in cutoff shorts and halter tops—unless they're men.

124.   Your college years can never be repeated. Don't waste much time on studying (unless you're some kind of genius and you plan to go on to even more school). The only think that matters is finishing—not what grades you get.

125.   Always give notice *after* collecting your Christmas bonus.

126.   Try to work only at night (or not at all, if possible). Days are best reserved for tanning and napping.

127.   Set aside any money given to your children in a special account. Then once they finish school, this money can be used for a trip around the world. Send them postcards from many places.

128.   Marry a women with a career. Otherwise you'll have to get one yourself.

129.   Don't encourage the teenage daughter of friends if she has a crush on you. Play hard to get—she won't lose interest as quickly.

130.   Just because the boss leaves early doesn't mean you should, too. Unless it can't get back to him.

131.   Never be the life of the party, but whoever it is, egg them on.

132.   Take Polaroid photos of your girlfriends in compromising positions. One of the women might become a celebrity some day, causing your photos of her to become very valuable. At the very least, after some years, you will have a fine collection to admire.

133.   Live beyond your means. If possible, well beyond.

134.   While at the beach bury bottlecaps and other worthless metallic junk in the sand. Return in the winter and watch when the old guys with the metal detectors think they've struck it rich.

135.   Generally speaking, you can ascertain a women's age by looking at the suntan lotion she uses. Under twenty: baby oil. Twenty to thirty: pink grease in an imported tube. Over thirty: assorted creams, ranging from total block down to something called "Number Six"—with separate extras for the nose, eyes, and lips.

136.   The older the woman, the bigger her purse.

137.   Borrow as much money as you can from relatives.

138.   Invite some vegetarians over for dinner. Throw some small pieces of meat into the vegetable stew, but don't mention it. Then watch as they swear up and down on the value of vegetables, saying they haven't felt this good in years.

139.   If you happen to dent a friend's car, return it to him (at night) without mentioning it. Chances are it will be a couple of days before he notices, and he'll assume it happened while it was parked.

140.   Put rum in your morning coffee.

141.   "No." Always means no...unless you just shelled out for really expensive dinner. Then it means "not yet." Keep trying!

142.   Get all of your stationery supplies from work.

143.   Acquire your linens while on vacation.

144.   See problems as problems. Don't let anyone fool you into thinking they are really opportunities. Opportunities are good; problems are bad. Any idiot should be able to tell them apart.

145.   Don't waste time doing work at home. You're not getting paid for it, no one sees it, and no one will remember it.

146.   Learn to remove all types of bras easily—and with one hand.

147.   Pay for motel rooms in cash.

148.   Avoid television programs consisting of old, fat, bald guys sitting around a table yelling at each other.

149.   Don't join a political party—unless you have reason to believe the F.B.I. is watching you. Then you join the Republican party.

150.   Support television programming that contains nudity, violence, and questionable language. Also cartoons.

151.   Don't give money to public television. It's only wasted on stupid shows that nobody watched even in England, where people could at least understand them.

152.   Don't give money to Jerry Lewis. After twenty years without a hit movie, he's still got a mansion, and nobody's closer to a cure for M.D. You figure it out.

153.   Encourage breast implants.

154. The early bird catches the worm. Sleep late and have pancakes. Also sausages, and those curly potatoes.

155. Visit Thailand.

156. If you have a car and most of your teeth, you'll be considered a catch by women at the laundromat.

157.   Never go to a movie that has subtitles.

158.   Don't waste much time reading books. If they're any good, eventually they'll be made into movies and then you can go watch them. And if they're no good, you sure don't want to suffer through reading page, after page, after page....

159.   Never buy a product because of a sexy model wearing a bathing suit. Advertising should not tease you into buying something you don't need. Wait until she is completely naked; then buy.

160.   Send away for one of those mail-order Oriental bride catalogues. Keep it handy for those times when your wife is behaving in a manner you don't consider suitable. One look at Soon Li's picture with the caption "I feel I've been put on the earth to please my husband in every way," and your wife will quiet right down.

161.   Don't buy a house until you are rich. Cleaning gutters and cutting grass can seriously cut into your weekend time for drinking beer while lying on the couch and watching T.V. Those tasks are best left to professionals, and they're expensive.

162.   Buy holiday gifts that come fully assembled.

163. Furniture is a complete waste of money, but one that wives do insist upon. A couple of lawn chairs and tables can be an excellent compromise. They're inexpensive, they provide seating, and they are fully mobile, so you can bring them from room to room, thus sparing you the expense of furnishing each room individually.

164. Always order a drink at a business meeting, even if nobody else does. Chances are your colleagues are just waiting to see what everyone else orders. Once someone "breaks the ice," they'll all jump right in; or at the very least, they'll have a drink when the second round comes up. And if they don't drink at all, it's best to learn that early so you can discontinue doing business with such types.

165. The drink of choice for a business lunch is scotch and water. In the case of a particularly important meeting, you might want to refrain from drinking scotch and water. In that case, stick with beer and shots.

166. Have a good bookie.

167. Learn to shoot pool.

168.   Frequent bars featuring entertainment of an adult variety.

169.   Go to local high school football games. It's a good way to get a sense of community...and meet cheerleaders.

170.   When choosing between two girls, always try for the prettier one. Generally speaking, the better looking a girl is, the dumber she will be. It might not be very fashionable to say, but it's a fact: The more physical gifts one is blessed with, the less brains one must develop. A lot of really gorgeous girls can slide right through life without ever learning a single thing. So most of the time the really stunning girls will be far easier to impress than those who are merely attractive.

171. Stay away from bars that have many motorcycles showing a lot of chrome lined up out front.

172. Try to arrange it so that you are out of town during the holidays. The amount you will save on tips (mailman, garbageman, etc.) will practically cover the cost of your trip.

173. Go to one of those places where you can cut your own Christmas tree. Just make sure you park out of sight, wear dark clothes, and remember to bring a saw.

174. If you find a gold watch on the floor of a large casino, pick it up and walk to the lost-and-found office. If anyone saw you pick it up and then followed you, they will think you turned it in. Once you're inside the office, stick the watch in your pocket and ask for directions to the restroom.

175. Never take a job in a post office. If you must, then wear a bulletproof vest, and don't make fun of the guy who talks to himself.

176. Remember, when planning the untimely demise of a loved one, that life insurance does not pay for "suicide".

177.   Learn to fish. There is no better way to waste a day that should be spent working.

178.   Don't ever beat your boss's boss in golf. Don't beat your boss either—unless the three of you are playing together.

179.   Learn to bowl. Unless your wife is genuine white trash, she'll never come along, giving you Thursday nights free.

180.   Play poker on Tuesday nights.

181.   Take a date horseback-riding. 'Nuff said.

182.   Take a first date to an expensive restaurant. She will be trying to impress you with how little she eats and will probably order just a salad. So essentially you'll get to eat a gourmet meal and only pay for one, yet still be seen as a big spender. But do encourage her to drink; though costly, it's a fine investment.

183. Go to a restaurant ahead of time and give the maître d' twenty bucks. Tell him to act like you're a bigshot. This one can be very impressive to your date—or very embarrassing if he gets your name wrong.

184. Don't watch home-improvement shows on TV.

185. Don't watch any educational shows on TV.

186.   Resist anything even remotely educational.

187.   A deck with a telescope and a hot tub is one home improvement that will pay for itself.

188.   Give your secretary a list containing the dates of your wife's birthday, your anniversary, Mother's Day, etc. Tell her to send flowers or an appropriate gift when the time arrives.

189. Show your secretary lacy underwear you've bought for your wife. Hint that you're not really sure about the size, though she and your wife look to be around the same. Well maybe, she is just a bit smaller in the chest, you might add embarassedly, while looking down at the floor, for good measure. In five minutes, either she will be out of her clothes or you will be out of a job.

190. Never pay for your mistress's apartment.

191. The supermarket is a fine place to meet women. Don't overlook the checkout girls.

192.   Don't have sex with your boss's wife—unless she's the big boss's daughter.

193.   Don't go to restaurants with your mistress. Not for the obvious reasons, but because there is no need to spend the extra money on her anymore.

194.   Tell everyone you'll be out of town for Christmas. Then do all your shopping when everything is on sale after the holidays. Give out the gifts the following weekend when "you get back."

195.   Find a local kid who is into working on cars. Get him to do your repairs in exchange for your buying beer for him and his underage friends. Make them pay you for the beer, of course, since youngsters need to learn responsibility from adult role models.

196.   Give clothes and old furniture to charities that give out blank receipts.

197.   Talk to your kids about drugs. Sometimes kids know the best place to get them.

198. Don't ever bring call girls to your house, especially when your wife is at home.

199. When your company is going to have a sporting event, take several weeks and practice up. When the time comes to collect the trophy, pretend the company bowlathon was the first time you had ever laid eyes on a bowling ball.

200. Never divorce your wife in order to marry another women. You wouldn't trade one Hank Aaron for another Hank Aaron and half your collection, would you?

201.   Big-city bus stations are good places to meet teenage girls. Bring a stuffed animal.

202.   Don't floss. Running string through your teeth is not natural.

203.   Don't tease big, mean dogs—unless they are in a cage and there is no chance of ever seeing them again.

204.   Don't kick tiny yelping dogs...too hard.

205.   If your $1,200 South American talking jungle bird
        refuses to talk, get a cat.

206.   Remember that a woman is more than just the sum of
        her parts. Times have changed, and now women want
        to be judged on their brains *and* abilities—you know—
        as a whole person. This wreaks havoc on the classic
        "Ten Point System" used by men for centuries. The
        sum of her parts being the basis of this point system, it
        must now be modified to include things such as I.Q.,
        opinions, feelings, earning potential...you get the pic-
        ture. Under the "new system," you still start with the
        sum of her parts. Then add in earning potential, and
        from that subtract for opinions, thoughts, etc. For
        example, if she's extremely opinionated, a militant

feminist perhaps, you must subtract quite a bit. But if she's the type who doesn't have many opinions, and she keeps those few to herself, you don't take away much at all! At first glance, it might seem that Bella Abzug could score higher than a *Playboy* playmate. While occasionally a moose with a good job does slip through this is as rare as a voluptuous babe's scoring a four in the old system because her loose dress "added pounds." So while no system's perfect, it does have its own checks and balances. Take Bella Abzug. She might get high marks for earning potential, but the amount you'd need to subtract for her dopey opinions, politics, and activism (not to mention that annoying voice) would clearly be higher, leaving a negative score. This would then be subtracted from the sum of her parts, placing her final "rating" well into the negatives.

Where, then, does this leave today's supermodels? Well, yesterday's automatic "ten" now must be judged as a complete individual, and sometimes that's not in her favor. While blessed with near flawless beauty and seemingly unlimited earning potential, offset this against her brains, and it just might be enough to tip the balance in the other direction. And that's before you take into consideration just how spoiled this woman will be from a lifetime of getting whatever she wants from men. And don't forget how bad she'll be in the sack since she never really had to do anything special to keep a guy's interest except lie there and look beautiful. No, the outlook isn't so bright for the supermodel.

So who will do well? One group formerly over-looked—porn stars—will be on top, of the list, that is. Adding up the sum of their parts, most porn stars are sitting squarely in the eight to ten range. Their earning potential is very good; while not up there with the supermodels, these are independent women with excellent careers. Most porn stars don't have too many annoying opinions, those who do will have to lose some points. Also the risk of disease is a negative. However, these women are accustomed to pleasing men and your most hidden fantasies will probably seem as tame to her as a trip to Disneyland. She might even bring home a lovely coworker for you to fraternize with. Add in the bonus that there is little chance of her having a close-knit family, and you've got a very high score. Close to perfect. So thanks to feminism, we've shifted our long-standing ideal away from yesterday's plastic beauty queen, to today, where a women is judged more completely on all of her attributes. And so the porn star rightfully emerges to the forefront of the feminine ideal. High time.

207.   Screen your calls.

208. Learn to play the guitar or piano, since most women love musicians. Instruments to avoid are the accordian, viola, French horn, and tuba.

209. Don't waste your money on a psychiatrist. Do you really think anyone you pay $100 an hour—twice a week—is going to tell you the truth? Of course all of your problems are going to be your parents' fault.

210. Learn to skin and butcher game animals.

211.   Don't drink beer when you're hunting—brandy is much better for keeping warm.

212.   Learn to start a fire under adverse conditions—for instance, blind drunk and in the dark.

213.   Teach your children to swim early. This will allow you to ignore them while you're at the beach. Also, you'll have a better chance to interact with young lifeguard and swim-instructor types.

214. Hire an *au pair* girl to help your wife with the kids. Preferably a blond one from a Scandinavian country.

215. Don't tell your friends you hate their kids.

216. Don't leaf through explicit pornography during family get-togethers—unless you're from Appalachia.

217.   Wear a conservative suit when on trial.

218.   Steer clear of federal witness relocation programs. The government can't even sell arms to foreigners without bungling the job. How the hell are they going to be able to protect you?

219.   Never visit a big city unarmed.

220.   Don't give your kids chemistry sets as gifts. They will find a combination of chemicals that explodes, regardless of what it says on the box.

221.   When you leave an amusement park, take all of your extra tickets and stuffed prizes; then find a nice little kid and sell them to him.

222.   Learn to spit well and far.

223.   Patronize resorts that allow thong bathing suits.

224.   A bad hangover can really spoil a vacation—the trick is
         to avoid getting one to begin with. This is best accom-
         plished by staying drunk.

225.   Don't try to smuggle anything through customs. In-
         stead, mail it to your boss at the office. When you
         return there, just ask him to give you the package. If,
         upon getting back, you find your boss is in a federal
         prison, consider it a good time to ask for a promotion.

226.   Avoid responsibility.

227.   Make a practice of taking long lunches, say, three or four hours. That way, when things get really busy and your coworkers are eating at their desks, you can cut lunch down to two hours and it will seem as though you're pitching in.

228.   Don't give *money* to homeless people. Walk with them to the nearest liquor store and buy them a bottle of cheap booze. They might use money for something other than booze—like food, maybe—and then the next time you see them, they'll be strong and sober, and probably very angry, too. If we all contribute, we can keep them drunk and happy. Sometimes worthwhile things take just a bit of extra effort!

229.   Whenever possible, urinate outdoors.

230.   Wash vegetables well. Then throw them out and have a steak.

231.   Never go to a ballet or an opera.

232.	When meeting a woman and trying to impress her with your sensitivity, no matter how tempting, never tell her you like the opera or the ballet. If you do, you will no doubt soon find yourself sitting through one.

233.	Always stop and run after children who throw snowballs at your car. Do it for *them*. Remember: Half the excitement was knowing you could get caught.

234.	As your kids get older, gradually increase their household responsibilities and chores. This will insure that they move out at their first opportunity.

235.   If you ignore problems, eventually they will disappear.

236.   Get a shave and a haircut before a court date.

237.   Ignore advice from older relatives. If they were so smart, they would be bigshot tycoons, and everyone would be interested in what they had to say. If by chance they *are* bigshot tycoons, still ignore their advice; just pretend to be interested.

238.   When lying, don't say, "To tell you the truth..." or "To be perfectly honest..."

239.   In business, take time to develop trust. These colleagues will be the easiest to take advantage of when an opportunity arises.

240.   The more resistance you put up, the less likely they will ask you for help the next time.

241. Don't get married until you are absolutely sure you are going to be a failure.

242. Get divorced before fame and fortune hit.

243. Learn to work around the clock. For instance, when the clock reads 10:00, it's coffee time; 12:00–3:30 is reserved for lunch. Haircuts are at 4:00, drinks at 5:00, and dinner at 6:30.

244.   When planning a family trip, spread a large map of the world out on a wall. Each family member then throws a dart at the map. Continue this until somebody hits Disney World. That's where you're going anyway. Who are you kidding?

245.   When your mother-in-law calls, tell her that you've been having trouble with the phone and the lines are being repaired. When she starts to annoy you, hang up on her. Don't answer the phone for the remainder of the day.

246.   When insurance salesmen call you at home, cough and wheeze a lot on the phone. Then tell them you're so glad they called because you really want to get health and life insurance, but you keep getting turned down and you can't get anyone to return your calls. Hello, Hello...

247.   If you find out your wife suffers from seasickness, profess a lifelong desire to take a cruise. If she stays home, you'll be a seaside bachelor for two weeks and have the time of your life. If she goes with you, and she probably will (since not many wives would give up the chance of an expensive trip, even if it meant nausea, vomitting, and diarrhea), chances are she'll be so busy throwing up, you'll be a seaside bachelor for two weeks and have the time of your life.

248.   In moments of rare tenderness you may find yourself compelled to tell your wife about a past indiscretion. DON'T. Such ideas are always far better in theory than in practice.

249.   When in doubt, keep your mouth shut; what you say can only come back to haunt you.

250.   Always keep a couple of crisp new $100 bills in your wallet right next to your driver's license. These will make talking with anyone in a position of authority go considerably smoother.

251.   Patronize bars with scantily clad cocktail waitresses.

252.   Use handicapped parking spots; they are usually empty anyway.

253.   Choose an accountant who used to work for the I.R.S.

254.   Choose a lawyer whom you could beat up.

255.   Choose a dentist from the yellow pages.

256.   Choose a vet that—naw, just get a new cat. It'll be cheaper.

257.   Don't get a car with a stick shift.

258.   That women have far a keener sense of smell than men is something to consider when you plan to have an affair in your home or car.

259.   The worse your behavior, the bigger the tip should be.

260.   There are many psychotic women out there. Learn to recognize them.

261.   Throw water balloons out of hotel windows.

262.   Dial 911 only in the case of an emergency. A loud party given by a particularly annoying neighbor *does* constitute an emergency.

263.   If you're planning to break off a long relationship, it's usually a good idea to have the moment of truth coincide with that dental surgery you've been avoiding. Things are going to be difficult for a week or two anyway, and this way you won't spoil a perfectly good week later on with the surgery. Also, the dental pain might make you a little more convincing when you tell her how much the breakup hurts you. As an added bonus, you'll be so knocked out from painkillers that the scene will be over before you know it.

264.   Never flirt with the wife of a gangster.

265.   Avoid nudist resorts—exhibitionism spoils voyeurism. Besides, these places are filled with fat, wrinkled old broads who no one wants to look at anyway.

266.   Try never to use public transportation.

267.   Memorize a couple of old poems and recite them as your own after bringing a date home.

268. Don't buy hats—unless they are wool and for warmth. Any hat you but for reasons of fashion will sit in your closet unworn, or would be better off that way. Particularly stupid looking are cowboy hats worn by non-cowboy city types. Or berets worn by anyone. Berets even look stupid on French guys, who are supposed to be wearing them.

269. Try to hire veterans. Utilizing their special talents can be tricky, though. It *does* help if you have a business that concentrates on going into other countries and wiping out their armies. But even if you don't, try to retrain the veterans to meet your needs. For instance, accounts receivable is a department in which a man trained to kill could be quite handy.

270. A painting is art if it looks remotely like what it is supposed to be. Multicolored smears of paint or forks with their tines bent and stapled to a canvas are not art, regardless of what anybody tells you.

271.   When in jail, don't correct grammatical errors made by the other inmates.

272.   As your children are growing up, have them sign IOU's for food, clothes, medical bills, vacations, toys, etc. If by some fluke they become tremendously successful and won't give you any money or return your calls, you'll have all you need to begin legal proceedings.

273.   Have your parents sign their house over to you. This way they won't lose it when they accrue medical and nursing home bills later in life. Which they undoubtedly will, since living on the streets does take its toll.

274.	Marriage is about trying to kill the other person's zest for life as quickly as possible. So in reality lifelong marriages are a complete failure. The successful marriage should only take year, or two tops, to complete.

275.	Invite some homeless people over for a holiday dinner—but give them a neighbor's address.

276.	Rush into marriage; it's definitely something that should be done while you still like each other.

277.   If you should find yourself visiting New York, avoid the theatre. Despite what some say, Broadway's not "worth a look," particularly when you figure in the $100 a ticket they get for most shows. In fact, there is no job less necessary than that of Theatre Critic, for the simple reason that all Broadway plays stink. What are they going to write—that the play with the signing hunchbacks is even more inane than the one with the singing cats? Not if they want to keep their jobs. And wouldn't you like to get up at the crack of noon, write out a review of the mess you fought to retain consciousness through the night before, have lunch, make a quick stop by the newspaper to drop off your column ...and back home for a nap. Then upon waking, meet your equally obnoxious friends for dinner at a pretentious little restaurant that serves tiny portions of crabmeat stuffed into macaroni, with a cold sauce made from mustard, leeks, and ginger ale. Then it's rush, rush, rush to catch an 8:00 curtain.

It's a pretty good job by anyone's standards—pretty good but totally useless since all plays are terrible (it deserves repeating.) First, you can never understand anything the actors are saying, and when by some fluke you are sitting in the one seat that has good acoustics, it's so boring you find yourself wishing for the days of fighting to hear each word. At least then you were involved. And even when you do hear everything, and manage to stay awake, you still won't have a clue what the show's about.

This is a trick used by practically all playwrights today. They write plays that don't make any sense. They found that when people understood what they were saying, most thought it was stupid. And no one produces a stupid play. So the playwrights have learned to shift the stupidity from themselves onto the viewer. They do this by writing a play that's unintelligible, causing the viewer to think he's too dumb to get it. "Knowing" his own intelligence to be quite high, the viewer then assumes the play, which is beyond him, must be a work of *total genius*. It started when a playwright who, frustrated by his failures, wrote a play that made no sense at all. Remarkably, it became a big hit, an international success overnight. You see, the producer didn't want to seem dumb by admitting he didn't understand the play so he said he loved it. It made him *think* more than any play in years. He just neglected to say that all the thinking was an attempt to figure out what the hell was going on. So he produced it. And the critics—who are even dumber than the producers, but far more vain (imaging themselves intellectually on par with the playwrights)—loved it. They wrote reviews explaining hidden meanings and nuances that the rest of us might not be sophisticated enough to get. All of it was garbage, of course, as the play was complete gibberish to begin with. Everyone who then saw it told of its depth, its brilliance through its simplicity. Well, after a short time the playwright became a celebrity. Everything he said and did was considered brilliant. All because no one could understand his play.

About this time his old playwright friends started to figure things out. And when the press came around to interview them on the humble beginnings of this modern genius (how he got his start, if his friends had known he was special etc.) they pretended to have discussed the ideas from which this play had sprung. Being playwrights, they never actually came out and said he was a genius, but led people to believe he was—just the first in their group to find mainstream success—which may make him less of a genius than the rest, since, everyone knows the better the art, the harder it is to recognize. And so, at that time they all started on the path of writing plays that made absolutely no sense. Each one more convoluted than the last.

In no time at all, these playwrights, too, were the "toast of the town," each with a string of hits. Naturally this didn't work for everyone. Just the ones with wild hair, dressed all in black with the stupidest black shoes available (preferably with large unsightly buckles.) These types generally showed the necessary arrogance to make the theatre critics awestruck. A polite guy in a crewneck just couldn't pull it off, as the critics would think themselves superior, and have no problem saying his play made no sense. Also, the theme of the work should lie in an area that is appealing to these critics. Themes with sufficient appeal would include alternative lifestyles, inner turmoils, the evils of business, and anything with dancing.

Thus we are left with a legacy of theatre so bad that reviews need only to tell one thing, whether or not it's a musical. For as bad as dramas are, there's only one thing even more unbearable...and that's a musical.

278.   Never wave to kids on school buses. If by some chance their return waves don't soon turn to swearing and throwing stuff at your car, then the bus driver will get your license plate number and report it to the authorities as that of a potential child molester.

279.   When dating a girl still in high school, you'd best avoid telling her father you think you went to school with his older brother.

280.   When dating a girl still in high school, you shouldn't mention to her father that girls have no cellulite at such a young age—and you know because you've looked *everywhere* for it.

281.   When dating a much younger girl, and people ask you what you two have in common, tell them, "Nothing—that's why after we finish having sex, she plays with my daughter, who is in her class in school."

282.   When choosing a mate, remember that her breasts will stay the same, but her backside will only get bigger.

283.   Support equal pay for equal jobs. Do you want your wife to bring home less money than if she were a man? Think of the implications—while you're struggling to make payments on your Chevette, gay couples are living it up on Fire Island.

284. Starting a new job? Remember: The best time to go in for surgery is during that brief period of time when you're insured by both the old job and the new one. Think of this extra money as a "signing on" bonus.

285. Try to keep a tan year round.

286. Anyone who tells you they can't lose weight no matter what they eat is lying. In the photos of concentration camp survivors did *anyone* appear overweight?

287. Wallow in self-pity. Sure, there are people worse off than you, but there are also people doing better—far better. And which ones do you want to compare yourself to, the winners or the losers?

288. Shoot for the stars! Use a high-powered rifle with a telescopic sight. Go for the character actors, and directors, too.

289. Retire early, while you are still young enough to enjoy it.

290.   Don't volunteer.

291.   Don't join the army. They wake you up way too early
        and make you run.

292.   When with police, it's best to play dumb.

293.   Always tell girls in rock bands that you are a record producer.

294.   When money comes in, integrity goes out the window.

295.   Wear sunglasses.

296.   Go back to school—there's no finer place to meet women.

297.   If you move into a condo or an apartment, don't sign up for cable right away. Wait to deal directly with the cable repairman. Hooking you up might be as simple for him as flipping a switch and giving you an old cable box that just happened to be lying in the back of his truck. Most times this can be arranged "in the field" with a one-time charge of fifty dollars, saving you the bothersome inconvenience of having to call the office and formally sign up. Of course, if a new repairman takes over the route, you might find your service temporarily disconnected until new negotiations can take place.

298. At the supermarket choose plastic rather than paper bags. They can mean the difference between just two or as many as four trips from the car to the house. The only time you would go for the paper is if the checkout girl looks like Donna Dixon and is wearing a peace sign on her tie-dyed shirt.

299. Don't take rides on glass-bottom boats. Any wildlife you want to see is on the beach.

300. Never talk on cordless phones. Anybody with a radio can listen in.

301.   Always wear cologne. That way, when you have an
         extramarital affair, you can brush on a few dabs to hide
         the her smell on you. Your wife's "other-woman radar"
         won't be set off by your "new" sweet-smelling habit.

302.   Guidance counselors can be helpful, but you must be
         honest with them. If you're looking for a job that
         affords you plenty of spare time, pays tons of money,
         takes little effort, and causes young babes to go wild,
         they will recommend you become a movie or rock star.
         But if you don't tell them what you want, they will just
         look at your test scores and point you in the direction of
         your strengths. Don't you think Einstein would have
         preferred having teenage chicks screaming, "Albert,
         Albert!" while tearing off their clothes, to sitting at a
         desk with a notebook and a calculator all day? Sure he
         would, but when his guidance counselor asked him

what he would like to do with his life, Einstein just shrugged and said, "I don't know." It turned out he was strong in math.

303.   When she emerges from the bathroom fully dressed after spending more than an hour preparing for a big night out, ask her what she is going to wear.

304.   Don't use chopsticks.

305.   Always pick out the cheapest coffin available. In a couple of days it'll be underground and the only guy who'll see it there is already dead.

306.   Don't let friends drive drunk—unless it's snowing very
        hard. In that kind of weather they'd probably crash
        anyway.

307.   Never give money to a political party; instead, ask if
        you can bring the beer or some burgers.

308.   Don't shave your head—unless you're eighteen or
        almost bald anyway.

309.   Tell a woman she looks like she's lost some weight.

310.   Go to the track and bet on a long shot to win.

311.   Learn to count cards.

312.   Don't ever have a picture taken with your mistress.

313.   Look up several private detectives in the phone book and tell each of them that some strange woman has been impersonating your wife. Advise each one that if the woman tries to hire him to follow you, he should turn her down and call you immediately. Let him know you'll take care of him.

314.   Check your rearview mirror often.

315.   Don't ever allow a prostitute to tie you up, even if she comes highly recommended.

316.   Never ask for an autograph. Only a idiot would want another person's signature.

317.   If you see a celebrity, ask for an autograph. After it's handed to you, read it, then look up and say disappointedly, "Sorry, I thought you were someone else."

318.   At a strip joint try to sit one table back from the stage. The view is just as good, and you save substantially on dollar bills.

319.   When hunting, don't wear those stupid orange vests. While certainly not as bright as humans, animals, are smart enough to recognize that there is no such thing as a drunken orange animal carrying a gun naturally occurring in the wild.

320.   Don't visit foreign lands. If they were so terrific, great numbers of their natives wouldn't be trying to come here.

321.   In a pinch, a Hefty Bag over the head will make a fine halloween costume for a small child.

322.   Take a child to the playground. It's a fine way to meet *au pairs*.

323.   Get a full-body massage.

324.   Go to an accountant who is used frequently by crooks. Crooks love deductions and hate taxes.

325.   Most people have an innate urge to collect things. Resist yours. And if you can't resist it, keep it to yourself— nobody is interested in your stamps or beer mugs.

326.   Own a business that deals in cash.

327.   When a stylish night club announces over the speaker system that a red Firenza with its lights on is parked in the lot, reach over and tap the shoulder of that gorgeous blond next to you. When she turns around, undoubtedly with a smug look on her face and a hostile tone in her voice, annoyed that you'd interrupt her while she was obviously engaged in an important conversation, ask her, "Did they just say something about a red Ferrari?" When she tells you they said "red Firenza," just say thank you, and quickly turn back away from her. Be sure you're wearing a watch with a sweep second hand, though, since you'll want to time just how long it takes her to drop the important conversation and tug at your sleeve, asking in an altogether different tone of voice, this one dripping with honey, all the while batting her eyelashes, "Do you really have a Ferrari?" It will be under a minute, in fact usually under thirty seconds—well under.

328.   Remember you are who you associate with. Elvis would still be here today if his entourage had a collective I.Q. higher than that of a prune danish.

329.   When speaking with someone who spits as he talks, taking a step back while wiping your face with your hand will generally give him an appropriate message.

330.   Don't accept collect calls.

331.   While visiting friends try to make some small talk
        before you head for their refrigerator.

332.   Turn off your headlights when you're being followed.

333.   Softball is for fat, drunken losers; don't play. And
        especially don't watch, unless it's a charity game be-
        tween teams of "Playmates."

334. The Grand Canyon is just a mountain gully, albeit a big one. Don't bother planning a trip around it.

335. Try to spend more time communicating with your wife. If you can't think of anything to say, just make stuff up, the sappier the better. Women love sappy talk, particularly about them. Avoid sappy talk about other women.

336. Alone with the babysitter? Act clumsy and adorable. She'll think she's the one who initiated things and feel so guilty for corrupting your marriage that she'll never try to get serious. She'll just concentrate on the kid, while giving you great sex to ease her guilt. Just don't ever let her catch you looking at another woman. Oh, yeah, and keep her away from your wife when you're not around.

337.   Behind hundreds of doors in condo developments there are women who are dying for it. Sometimes all you have to do is knock, but most times you'll need to make up a pretty good story when they answer.

338.   The ten semifinalists in the Miss America contest should mud wrestle for the crown. Then they should answer the question "If you can choose to be anyone in the world, living or dead, who would you choose to be, and why?"—while still in their G-strings and bikini tops, and covered with mud.

339.   How do you know if you are a success in life? First, examine your relationships. If you are still not sure, next look to your work life. Are you satisfied, are you respected, are you still a caddy living with your mother?

340.   Remember that everyone is selfishly motivated. Don't
        feel guilty for tossing out the resumé of the applicant
        who has thirty years of experience, takes steno, and
        types 120 words a minute—while you keep the one of
        the twenty-two-year-old applicant, who briefly attended
        secretarial school, hand-wrote her resumé (dotting the
        i's with little hearts), thinks of herself as a "people
        person," and interviewed braless.

341.   Learn to shoot craps.

342.   Keep a bible in your house. It serves many functions,
        not the least of which is giving you some respectability
        in the eyes of the F.B.I. agents who search it.

343.   When entering a brothel, leave your wallet in the car.

344.   Don't tell a women you just met that you're dying to see her naked.

345.   Take family vacations by car, preferably station wagons with vinyl seats and no air-conditioning. Go in August.

346. Camping is just another way of saying "sleeping outside." This is what homeless people do. Homeless people sleep outside not for the pleasure it affords them, but because they have to. Given a choice, most homeless people would opt for a night at the Ritz Carlton with room service, over an evening "under the stars." And if you insist upon seeing stars most fine hotels will offer a balcony—after gazing heavenward for a minute or two you can go back inside, flop down on the king-size bed, and watch more stars on close to eighty cable channels (not to mention pay-per-view movies of an adult nature). Even better, you can leave your empty vodka bottles, Cheeto bags, and cigarette butts where they fall with no feelings of guilt. If you were camping, this would be considered littering, a sin of the largest proportion. In a hotel however, the same act qualifies you as a capitalist, since you will be helping to build the economy by creating jobs for maids and by fueling the

demand for cleaning products, vacuum bags, and tiny bars of soap. And if you're capitalist, hotel stays are a tax write-off. They're simply seen as a necessary business expense and are thus fully deductible. So if you must travel, sleep inside. They best place is a four-star hotel, next would be a three-star, followed by a two-star, etc. After the hotels, your best bet is a motel, then a motor inn, and finally, as a last resort, a country inn or bed-and-breakfast. Only after all of these (indoor) options have been explored should you consider camping.

347.   Don't get tattoos. Today's cool is tomorrow's identifiable mark.

348.   When in Rome, do as...best as you can to get back to America.

349. Enjoy colorized movies, and laugh at anyone else who thinks it's a crime to ruin a "work of art" in such a manner.

350. Stamp all hospital bills DECEASED; then throw them back in the mailbox.

351. FINAL NOTICE written on a bill is no cause for alarm. True final notice comes in the form of a 350-pound guy named "Tiny" banging at your door with sausagelike fingers protruding from gloves cut off at the first knuckle. This is the time to pay, since guys like Tiny normally won't offer an extension. Also noteworthy: They seldom take checks.

352.   It counts as cheating only if you get caught.

353.   Animals have rights—the rights to be steaks, chops, coats, hats, and gloves.

354.   Don't drink spritzers.

355.   Cover your tracks.

356.   When meeting a new group of people, you can never remember all of their names, so try to concentrate instead on a select few. This way, later on, when you goof up, you won't alienate everyone. Try to focus on the ones who can do the most for you.

357.   Integrity is for people who never get anywhere.

358.   If you get a chance to endorse a product, first make sure it's going to be something that pays well.

359.   Keep a pair of gloves in your car.

360.   Sports figures are stupid, sports writers are more stupider, and sports fans are stupidest of all.

361.   Don't ever trust people who sell things.

362.   The better her body, the more devious she will be.

363.   Need a great deal of money in a hurry? Try burning
        down your house for the insurance. Just be sure to get
        all your valuables taken out and hidden away first.
        Also, the inspectors aren't stupid, so try to avoid
        leaving too many empty gas cans lying around. And be
        sure to "tip" the fire inspector handsomely for a job
        well done; ten to fifteen percent of the insurance
        settlement is customary (for a report reading "No
        evidence of foul play"). If this seems a bit steep, and you
        want to try keeping your expenses to a minimum,
        threatening the inspector's life will often work just as
        well, and it won't cost you a dime.

364.   Encourage your wife to find hobbies she enjoys. This will give you extra time for diversions of your own. An added bonus: You'll get points for being "supportive."

365.   Always apply to a college that is below your abilities. Better to be the smartest in a group of dopes, than the dumbest in a group of scholars.

366.   Don't quote from Shakespeare—you will alienate many more than you will impress. Those whom you *do* impress will be so pompous that you'd do better without them.

367.   Don't quit your job to do something more meaningful.
        Quit for another job that pays more, or quit because
        you hate it.

368.   Always light a fire when you bring women home. If you
        don't have a fireplace, a 55-gallon drum next to an open
        window will do fine—unless you own the place. Then
        just light some candles.

369.   Remember, out on a date a girl is looking for things she
        can tell her friends to impress them. No girl wants to
        have sex with a guy who makes her friends go "ugh."
        She wants them to be jealous of her. Win the friends,
        win the girl. It's as simple as that.

370. A girl who does not wear panties on the first date is a girl you want to go out with again.

371. For almost any article you will find in a magazine, you will find another article telling you exactly the opposite. Save your time and just look at the pictures.

372. Learn to write with your opposite hand. "Most Wanted" bulletins usually specify right- or left-handed.

373.　　When out to dinner with other couples, always order your drink last. This way you'll know what to have. If the other guys in the group order piña coladas or white wine spritzers, you can order lite beer and still appear very masculine. However, If you order a lite beer first, one of the others might order bourbon or scotch, leaving you looking—well, let's just say a tad on the girlish side. If you find yourself in a bind and, you *must* order first, always go with a double Wild Turkey, straight up. A double Wild Turkey is a drink that for sheer manliness cannot be beaten; at best it can be tied. But a double Wild Turkey, straight up and ordered first, can not even be tied. Anyone else who orders the same drink or something similar after you will appear only to be trying to look manly and keep up. And how can someone so calculating as that be taken for anything but a buffoon?

374.　　Drink your coffee black.

375. If you smoke, go with the unfiltered variety.

376. Never, ever strike your kids—unless they misbehave.

377. Videos of your kids are today's equivalent of yesterday's home movies. It may be easier just to pop the cassette into the VCR and press play than it was to thread the projector, set up a screen, and splice broken fragments of film back together. But just because videos are easy to handle, that doesn't make them any less boring to your friends and neighbors. The fact that your parents raved about them doesn't make them good. Remember what your mother said the first time she was confronted with your kid's dirty diaper? She thought that was a work of art, too.

378. Don't drink cappuccino and don't buy any machines to make it, either. Along with yogurt makers, coffee grinders, pasta makers, ice cream makers, and waffle irons, these devices invariably require ten minutes' cleaning time for each minute of operation and still make an end product far inferior to any sold commercially.

379. Videotape your girlfriend in the bathtub. Make sure the camera is completely out of sight, since girlfriends tend to become irate if they catch you. These tapes are very valuable; sell or trade them with friends.

380. Visit a commune. Don't do any work, though. Just hang out freeloading until they throw you out. If you wanted to work, you could just stay at your job where they pay you for it.

381.　Buy an ice-cream cone for a date. Make suggestive remarks while she eating it.

382.　Blondes have more fun, but brunettes give more. And redheads give the most of all.

383.　Show respect to military men—they have guns. Show respect to anyone who has a gun.

384.   If, after you've been married for ten years, your
        mistress shows you a new trick in bed, don't rush home
        and show it to your wife.

385.   When a cop is behind you, keep your eyes out of the
        rearview mirror, and don't go too slow. Also, don't
        scramble around looking for something and then hide it
        under the seat or toss it out the window once you've
        found it.

386.   When pulled over by a state trooper, keep both hands
        on the wheel—unless you're a wanted fugitive on the
        lam. In that case, keep your left hand on the wheel and
        your right on your gun. Also, if possible, don't pull over
        in the first place.

387.   In prison don't ever volunteer for a part in the female impersonator show.

388.   When starting a small business, it's best to ignore as many federal regulations as possible—state and local, too.

389.   When fitness is the goal, remember that aerobics might build a healthy heart, reduce cholesterol, and increase longevity, but it's weight lifting that gives you those impressive arms.

390. Inspect your pornography for those loose subscription cards. Then gather and burn them. This can save you considerable embarrassment by preventing a card from the super summer issue of *Jumbo Jugg Digest* from falling to the floor unbeknownst to you, only later to be found by your wife.

391. Pyramid schemes never work—unless you get in early.

392. If you can't find time to work out, take a few minutes and watch an exercise show on TV. A couple of minutes watching those leotard-clad beauties should get your heat rate into the target range, your breathing heavier, and work up a slight sweat.

393.   Your in-laws are not your enemy. Your wife is your enemy; your in-laws are merely her allies.

394.   Just for fun, the day before Halloween go to a small, family-owned market and buy a package of razor blades and a couple of dozen apples. For good measure act, annoyed at the children of the woman in line in front of you.

395.   Don't let your girlfriend dance in stiletto heels on your waterbed.

396.   Invite in any attractive young girls bearing petitions
        who come knocking at your door. Offer them coffee.
        Act really interested in the dumping of nuclear waste
        into public swimming pools, or whatever it is they are
        trying to stop, or start, as the case may be. If they want
        money, tell them that you're broke now, since you just
        gave all your savings to Greenpeace to stop the needless
        slaughter of innocent beavers. Ask her if she'd like
        something to eat—after all, you don't want the food in
        the fridge to spoil, and you haven't been able to eat any
        of it yourself since you heard about the starvation of the
        Ecuadorian refugees. Worst comes to worst, she'll cook
        you dinner, but quite possibly the interest on your
        beaver investment just might come due.

        If it's a young girl *selling* something at your door,
        things will be considerably easier. No need for a
        bleeding-heart story, just tell her you'll buy *two* if she'll
        have sex with you. Free trade has its perks.

397. Of all the words of tongue and pen the saddest are these: We've got you on videotape.

398. Don't say "could have" and "should have." Instead say "could've" and "should've."

399. Don't have pets fixed. Buy ones that are undamaged to begin with.

400. When a young women in a miniskirt and high heels comes up to your car while you're stopped for a red light and asks you if you'd like a date, she is *not* referring to an evening at the opera followed by a cozy dinner.

401. Don't take your wife for granted. Don't take her anywhere at all.

402. Don't buy one of those watches that makes beeping sounds.

403. Get a beeper and wear it on your belt. Chicks will think you have an important job, like a doctor or a business executive. Add sunglasses to look really important, like a drug kingpin.

404. No one likes the last guy on the block to rake the leaves and shovel the walk. The only guy they like less is the first one.

405. Don't buy a snowblower; if the snow is too deep for a shovel, go back to sleep until everything melts.

406.   During long car trips, the woods are always preferable
        to public restrooms. Unless you're in hillbilly country,
        in which case you'd do best to hold it in.

407.   There are Swiss banks as close as the Bahamas.

408.   Never pay for more than half of an abortion. How will
        she ever learn her lesson if you bail her out?

409.   If you work for a credit card company, call the people who have *very large* outstanding balances. Tell them that if they pay you $1000.00 cash, you will erase any balance showing on their account. Call as many customers as you can. Try to set up several hundred who are willing to go along with you—but it's important you avoid mentioning your name. Have them to send the money to a P.O. box (one that you've opened under an alias) in another city. Do all the transactions in one month. It might take a bit of overtime, but nobody ever got anywhere without lots of good, honest hard work.

The next part—whether or not to clear their accounts—is up to you. If you *do* and the company finds out, they will go after you with all they've got. Unless, of course, they try to keep the whole thing quiet, in which case you're home free. But—if you don't clear their accounts, the company will have no reason to go after you, and the customers can't do anything. What are they going to do? Tell the police they gave somebody—

whose name they don't know—money to wipe out their balance? Doubtful. Besides the obvious legal implications, it makes them look pretty stupid.

But are you morally obligated to provide the service you offered? This is a tough one, and one only you can ultimately answer. On the one hand, you did make a deal, but they had already made a deal with the credit card company. So, technically, it is they who are guilty of bad faith for trying to worm out of their earlier obligations. For many of you, this will be reason enough not to clear their balances—let them get what they deserve for being so dishonest. Others of you will see this as sinking down to the customer's level in worming out of a deal already made. Also to be considered: How are these people ever going to learn to become financially responsible if you just wipe out their debts? They won't! And in the long run they'll only end up in the same mess, with no one to help them out the next time. But whatever you decide, the next step is to take all the money and leave the country.

410.   Don't donate your organs, sell them. They even get money for calves' liver, which nobody likes or needs. Your body parts should be worth considerably more.

411.   Frying foods locks in their flavor and nutrition. Use plenty of oil or lard.

412.   Always doubt the validity of statements favoring the safety of travel by air over that of travel by automobile. Maybe more people crash cars than planes, but they don't do it six miles up in the air.

413.   If you were supposed to read between the lines, they
        would put words there.

414.   A "good loser" is a loser.

415.   The fact that all movie critics are paid off helps to
        explain some of the good reviews given to dopey foreign
        movies.

416.   Don't let your wife have a bank account that doesn't require your signature for a withdrawal.

417.   Avoid visiting South American countries. While they may look very appealing in the travel guide photographs, the reality is much different. The pictures of tourists being taken away in handcuffs to be beaten with rubber hoses and have electrodes clamped to their nipples—after a full cavity search—seldom make the brochure.

418.   Keep all firearms fully loaded and easily accessible.

419.   Women may like men who are sensitive, but they love men who are animals.

420.   Don't take any courses. If you have a talent or interest in an area, just go with it. Taking classes will only destroy any natural style you possess. Generally, the teacher will be a frustrated _____. (Fill this in according to what the class teaches, i.e., if it's a pottery class, a frustrated potter; if it's a sculpting class—you get the point.) And if you have any talent, he will only try squelch it. Of course this squelching will be disguised as helping you to learn "the fundamentals," and "basic techniques." Fundamentals and basic techniques are designed to get you so frustrated that you soon begin to question whether or not you really have any ability at all—ability in an area that two weeks ago you were certain was going to become your life's work. He'll destroy your zest for origami by insisting you stop

making exotic jungle birds with colorful paper and instead practice folding pieces of cardboard in half and diagonally until he thinks you're ready to move on. Which is usually when it is time to sign up for Origami Two—at the conclusion of which, any of the initial joy and excitement should have been beaten out of you, leaving you a robot who can no longer think for himself, but can only do from rote as was learned.

421.   Never get involved in any form of local government— unless you own a plumbing business and all the bathrooms in the municipal buildings are ready to be replaced.

422.   In for surgery? Always hit on the least attractive nurse; she's the one who is normally left alone. You can expect a response of grateful receptiveness.

423.   When you're flattering a woman, sincerity is always best. This can best be accomplished by looking misty-eyed and stammering. Blushing from embarassment is good, too.

424.   Stay out of bad neighborhoods—unless you need drugs or a hooker; in that case, they're among the best places to look.

425.   Don't ever kill in anger. Instead, hire someone to do it for you while you establish an alibi. Then when it's time to pay off the killer, meet him and kill him instead.

426.   Lavishly tip everyone with whom you come into contact on a regular basis. In the future, this will only help if you need someone to remember having seen you on a specific day, a day when the police might think you were...say, in another state committing a felony.

427.   Don't let your boss catch you with your fingers in the cookie jar. Or his secretary.

428.   Do business with people who give you lavish gifts and cash bribes.

429. Enjoy the freeze-frame feature on your VCR while viewing porno movies.

430. In the afternoon, frequent motels that have parking lots well concealed from the main road.

431. Tell high school cheerleaders they have a lot to offer that most guys never take the time to see—because they are too busy looking at what's on the outside.

432. Don't bother hitting on Vegas cocktail waitresses. Unless you are playing with $100 chips, they won't be interested. If you are playing with $500 chips and betting lots of them each hand, you can pretty much do whatever you like. Interested or not, they'll be all over you. The pit boss will see to it.

433. Don't eat octopus. Or squid. Or sushi. You don't eat bait, do you?

434. When in foreign countries don't make any attempt to speak their language. If they want the American tourist's dollar, they can at least make the effort to speak our language.

435.   The average person in this country watches 34 hours of television a week. This is clearly too much—unless of course videos and the dirty-movie channel are included, in which case the viewer is showing remarkable restraint and could probably add six to ten hours to that total easily.

436.   Try to dump your wife before you cash in the lotto ticket.

437.   Don't trust people who repair electronic items, particularly those who speak with accents.

438.　Don't put money in parking meters.

439.　Call women executives "sweetheart" and "honey"; they really seem to like that.

440.　Don't ever hold up a convenience store or bank. No matter how bad things seem, it's just not worth it. Besides, they have those cameras.

441.   Don't use mousse.

442.   If you are going to buy a Jaguar, buy two. This way you'll have one to drive while the other one is in the shop.

443.   Don't teach your hobbies to your girlfriend. As good an idea as it might seem at the time, in the future she may be your wife, and then, looking back, you will realize what a mistake it was—especially as she consistently beats you in golf.

444.   Set your car-radio buttons to a variety of different stations from classical to jazz, rock to new wave. This will impress almost any type of woman you care to take for a ride. Avoid top-forty stations, since you wouldn't want any woman in your car who is a top-forty fan anyway. You might have to make an exception and program one in, should you begin to date a high school cheerleader. A man has to learn when to compromise his values for the greater good.

445.   Remember, stopping payment on a check costs only $15, which is something to consider when the purchase price of the item the check was written for is several hundred.

446.   Always remember to remove your shades when traveling through customs.

447.   Memorize the names of famous authors and their books for impressive cocktail party banter. A good, basic idea of the plot, though not necessary, is always helpful.

448.   Between you and a coworker for a promotion based on a three-month-long project coming to a head? A refrigerator magnet shoved under their computer, which will erase everything the next time it's turned on, might be just the thing to swing things in your favor.

449.   Go to a museum and start conversations with attractive ladies regarding the artwork. You will find yourself more successful if you wear a turtleneck and a sports-coat with elbow patches.

450.   Bring liquor to hotel rooms. A room-service charge for a bottle of vodka will often be eight times the price it sells for in a liquor store. This can cut severely into your entertainment budget, leaving little for dancers and hookers.

451.   If you find a gun hidden in one of your wife's shoe boxes, ask questions.

452.   Most guys who get divorced thought everything was going well. Take one night a week and try to find out how your wife feels about stuff. This is usually not as painful as it sounds and many times will end up in great sex. Your girlfriend should have no problem with your staying at home this one night; if she does, she is being selfish and unreasonable. Replace her.

453.   Don't ever invest money with your brother-in-law.

454.   Don't ever patronize the inherited business of a former
         classmate. Particularly one whose guts you once hated.

455.   Own a large parcel of wilderness land in another state.

166

456.	In crowded airplanes you can often get additional room by not shaving or showering for a day or two before departure. Reading an issue of *Buxom Blondes in Bondage* in your seat while loudly commenting on the photos also helps.

457.	Don't go to the Olympics. You will see more of the action on TV, pre-edited to remove the boring non-championship rounds, as well as those events dominated by foreigners. And it's free.

458.	Always ski on trails a notch or two below your ability. The babes on Buttermilk Basin will think you're an expert, while those on Avalanche Run will see you at your true ability level.

459.   Never rent a ski house without a hot tub. There is no better way to get ski bunnies back to your place than the casual mention of a hot tub while you're sharing a chair lift up the mountain.

460.   If you get rich, resist the urge to buy stuff for family members. They will never really appreciate it, soon come to expect it, and eventually resent you for it.

461.   Many commuter trains offer a bar car. Use it.

462.   A beer and a hardboiled egg are hardly a balanced lunch. All of your nutritional needs can be met, however, by adding in a shot of scotch.

463.   Sell your house without the aid of real estate brokers. They are vultures.

464.   If you own rental apartments, try to collect the rent in cash and deduct some of those "empty apartments" as a business loss.

465.   Don't eat in restaurants that are mob hangouts. Although the food will undoubtedly be excellent, the chance of the place being sprayed by machine-gun fire tends to be far greater than in other restaurants.

466.   Don't overlook parent-teacher night as an excellent chance to meet women—both teachers and mothers, as well as some of the more mature students.

467.   Don't buy Barbie dolls for boys.

468. Some people can never be happy with simple pleasures. They will always want to have more. You know the type: extremely organized, very neat, highly ambitious. Keep your associations with them limited. They make horrible bosses but very good employees; take advantage of them as such. The more they feel under scrutiny, the more they tend to produce. But, as bad as they are at being bosses, they are far worse as friends or spouses, so avoid them after hours. When they start to make comments and recommendations on your leadership style, you know it's time to dump them. Though they think otherwise, they're relatively easy to replace.

469. Never criticize the FBI in public.

470. Don't tell secrets to anyone—particularly women.

471.   Never pass up the chance to see a naked lady.

472.   Discourage overnight visitors, unless you are in the hotel business or it's an intoxicated young girl in high-heel shoes and a mini dress.

473.   If possible, marry a bisexual woman.

474.   If you are in a service business, don't do any work for lawyers.

475.   Don't take any trip that tries to make work sound like fun. Walking up at dawn to feed the chickens and milk the cows before breakfast might make interesting copy in the brochure, but it makes for lousy vacations. If it were so much fun, you wouldn't see so many farmers at Disneyland and Vegas. Also avoid boat trips where they make you do all the work sailing to an island, and have you sleeping under the stars on the deck (that is, if you're "off duty"). But the worst of these by far is the "spa" vacation. The spa vacation is one in which they wake you at dawn for calisthenics, followed by a breakfast of one egg white on a piece of dry toast—with all the carrots and celery sticks you can eat, neatly cut and displayed in drinking goblets on the table—*Bon appétit.*

After breakfast it's off to the gym for an aerobics class, then weight lifting (or rather body shaping) and a sauna before lunch. And what a lunch it is! One would never guess there were so many delicious ways of preparing four ounces of plain white fish served with all the brussel sprouts you can eat, and freshly filled goblets of carrot and celery sticks. Tempting as it might be, try not to gorge yourself too much, since you wouldn't want to get full and sleepy and miss the afternoon activities.

Starting with a big hairy guy punching and kneading at you while you lie naked on a big table—made worse by the fact that you feel obligated to make some sort of conversation with him. If you make it this far, your reward is a glass of juice made from the celery and carrot sticks leftover from breakfast and lunch. Then it's off to meditation. Translated: even this staff of Nazi

Barbies and Kens needs a rest, so why not get all the dopes (guests) to sit cross-legged on the floor chanting a nonexistant, two syllable word for an hour.

Dinner time. A Hawaiian theme tonight means four ounces of grilled chicken and a slice of pineapple. Oh, and a large dinner salad, with no dressing. But as bad as the dinner is, the conversation around the table is worse. You'll hear fat women who dream of brownies the way priests dream of Cub Scouts, saying how they prefer to eat this way. And if it weren't for their kids and stress, they'd eat this way all the time. (This from a woman whose biggest stress in life is leaving Bloomingdales a few minutes early so she can make her nail appointment.) All the while the men just look on and nod, waiting for the optional four ounces of white wine served with unbuttered popcorn during the after-dinner movie. Some of the men become equally enthusiastic, but most are counting the hours 'til this torture ends and they can go back to work. How much will such a getaway run you? About three times the price of visiting any place else in the world—for twice the length of time. So, if your wife insists, offer to send her. She'll love it.—and just think of what you can do with a free week at home...

476.   Don't try that William Tell shoot-the-apple-off-the-head trick. Not even when drunk. If by some chance you *do* get talked into doing it, insist on being the bow-and-arrow guy; try to avoid being the apple guy.

477.   Your children will not take care of the dog regardless of what they say when they beg you for one. Make sure your wife will—or get a turtle.

478.   If you become successful, rub it in everyone's face.

479.   Don't teach your wife to handle weapons.

480.   If you ever feel fat or ugly, visit Disney World.

481. As you leave a very popular movie and walk past the line waiting for the next show, discuss the surprise ending.

482. When you're on vacation, visit resorts. Pyramids and ruins are best seen in books.

483. Don't waste money on health insurance. Instead, put it into a mutual fund that invests in health-related stocks. By the time you get sick, you should have more than enough to cover your bills, plus some left over for a mansion, a swimming pool, and round-the-clock nursing care.

484.   Discipline is essential for success. Instill it in your children from an early age by giving them a schedule of chores for each week and insisting they finish them before doing anything else. This will teach them later in life not to put off work for momentary pleasures—and right now it'll give you plenty of time on the golf course or the hammock.

485.   Don't plant trees in the spring. If you do, you'll only have more leaves to rake or pay to have removed come the fall.

486.   Don't go to costume parties.

487.   If you fill out your Rolodex cards with a typewriter, you need therapy.

488.   Don't have cookouts in public parks. If you don't have a backyard or know someone who does, eat inside.

489.   Keep bad records. This makes it much easier to read things in your favor come tax time.

490.   Remember: The combination of hard work and a good attitude can get you to the top. A shortcut would be to marry the boss's daughter.

491.   When at a classical music concert, ask the eighty-year-old matron sitting beside you, "Who's coming out first: AC/DC, Mega Death, or Metalica?"

492.   Support the rating of motion pictures. Ratings are useful in making an informed decision as to whether or not to see a movie. For example, a movie can have a really hot advertising campaign, but you know that if it has a PG rating, the actress won't appear naked, so you should skip it and go see something else.

493.   Watch out for quiet neighbors that keep to themselves.

494.   Planning on moving? Sublet your apartment. Have
        your new tenant pay you in cash six months in advance.
        Don't mention this arrangement to your landlord.
        Leave no forwarding address.

495.   Place a personal ad in the newspaper describing your-
        self as an extremely handsome, wealthy, single male
        looking for that special someone for good times and
        possibly more. Insist on nude photos with any letters.
        "Handsome" and "wealthy" are key words for attract-
        ing responses. "Possibly more" is the tease that most
        women will need to get them to send the pictures. You'll
        be amazed, with dozens of fine photos to admire, along

with some letters of an exceedly intimate nature. The thought of limousines and unlimited credit cards ignite in women the type of passion normally reserved for men enticed by Swedish nursemaids, or dogs with coffee tables. Don't go out with any of them, though, since only a nut would send naked pictures of herself to a complete stranger.

496.   Always hit on the woman sitting next to you on a plane. How many times in life are you presented with a captive audience who cannot escape for several hours?

497.   Try to get the secretarial pool to wear bathing suits.

498.   Getting a tax audit? Try to rent a friend's or a neighbor's children for a couple of weeks. Little Johnny and Ernestine, it turns out, aside from being just about as cute as a button (and saying the darnedest things), are nice, big, fat deductions. Any creative bookkeeping you've been doing that the IRS officials might catch can easily be offset by several children you've failed to deduct. The more tax owed, the more children you would need to borrow, in order to balance things in your favor. More than nineteen children, however, is not recommended, particularly if your apartment has only one bedroom and you're not married. The IRS officials just might get suspicious.

499.   Remember: Older women are a lot more experienced than young girls. There is a lot an older women can teach you—for instance, how to fill out those social security forms, or how to tell if a melon is ripe. But if

it's not hot action you're looking for, avoid the senior center, and try the student center.

500.   What do you do if your next-door neighbor is the spit and image of the guy being profiled on the *America's Most Wanted* show on TV? First thing—find out the size of the reward. Then decide if it's enough money to be worth jeopardizing your friendship (anything over $500 would qualify as an automatic yes). As a fringe benefit, he won't be borrowing of your power tools anymore while in a federal facility. Oh, yeah, it might be a good idea to hide your hacksaw blades—just until after his incarceration.

501.   Don't ever tell a female employee that she will get a promotion if she has sex with you—vaguely hint at it with ambiguous language.